The Maoris of New Zealand

The Maoris arrived in New Zealand about 1,200 years ago, traveling by canoe across the Pacific. For nearly 1,000 years, they lived their lives free from outside interference. The arrival of the Europeans in the eighteenth century brought struggles over land, culminating in the wars of the 1860s and '70s. Since then, there has been a slow but steady integration of white New Zealanders and Maoris and today they live in relative harmony. Graham Wiremu, who is himself part Maori, explains how and why these developments have taken place. He also tells why, in spite of the progress, problems still remain to be solved.

A colorful scene at a gathering on a marae. *Hundreds of visitors and a TV camera crew watch the celebrations.*

Original Peoples

THE MAORIS
OF NEW ZEALAND

Graham Wiremu

Rourke Publications, Inc.
Vero Beach, FL 32964

Original Peoples

Eskimos — The Inuit of the Arctic
Maoris of New Zealand
Aborigines of Australia
Plains Indians of North America
South Pacific Islanders
Indians of the Andes
Indians of the Amazon
Bushmen of Central Africa
Pygmies of Central Africa
Bedouin — The Nomads of the Desert
Zulus of Southern Africa
Lapps — Reindeer Herders of Lapland

Text © 1989 Rourke Publications, Inc.

Library of Congress Cataloging-in-Publication Data

Wiremu, Graham, 1950–
   The Maoris of New Zealand / Graham Wiremu.
      p.   cm.—(Original peoples)
   Reprint. Originally published: Hove, East Sussex, England : Wayland, 1985.
   Bibliography: p.
   Includes index
   Summary: Describes the history, culture, and daily life of the Maoris of New Zealand and how they are adjusting to a changing world.
      ISBN 0–86625–264–9
   1. Maoris—Juvenile literature. [1. Maoris. 2. New Zealand.]   I. Title.   II. Series.
[DU423.A1W57 1989]
993.1'004994—dc19
                                    88–15071
                                       CIP
                                       AC

Printed in Italy by Tipolitografia G. Canale & C. S.p.A. - Turin

Contents

Introduction

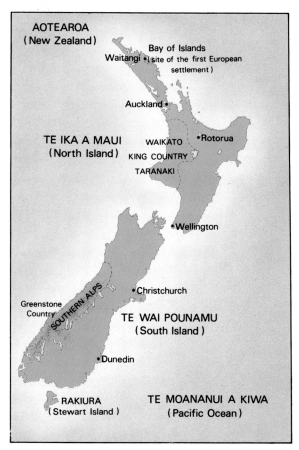

New Zealand is a small country consisting of two large islands and a number of smaller ones. It is situated far south in the Pacific Ocean. During the nineteenth century many thousands of people — mainly from the British Isles — went there to live. They formed a new nation, and as a result the language, laws, customs and lifestyles of New Zealand are very like those of Britain itself. In fact, New Zealand has more pipe bands than there are in Scotland!

Before these settlers arrived, another race of people were already living in New Zealand — the Maoris.

Until just over 200 years ago they had the land to themselves. Away from contact with other people — Australia, many hundreds of miles away, is the nearest large country — the Maoris evolved a unique culture and way of life.

When the settlers arrived from Europe they created many problems for the Maoris, resulting in war, disease and the loss of most of their land. The Maoris were soon outnumbered and had to adapt to their traditional ways in order to survive.

The head of a Maori weapon — a taiaha.

The rangatira *(chief) addresses his people on the* marae — *the central open space in a Maori village.*

They *have* survived as a people, and much of their distinctive culture has survived with them. Today, Maoris speak English, wear the same sort of clothes and live in the same kind of houses as other New Zealanders. Nevertheless, they often have different ideas and beliefs and are aware of their different history and background.

This book tells the fascinating story of the Maoris — of their origins, how they lived before the Europeans came and how they live now, and how they fought for their land and freedom. It also tells of the difficulties they have faced in adjusting to the modern world and the remarkable way in which they have succeeded.

7

Chapter 1 **Vikings of the sunrise**

Who are the Maoris?

Until about 1,000 years ago there were no humans living in New Zealand. Then the first canoes arrived, bringing the first people. We will never be quite sure exactly when or why these first Maoris went to New Zealand. From the work of archaeologists and other scientists, and from the ancient stories of the Maoris themselves, we have been able to find some pieces of the puzzle.

The Pacific Ocean showing the area explored by the Polynesians. The people who settled in New Zealand came from the tropical islands of the vast Pacific region.

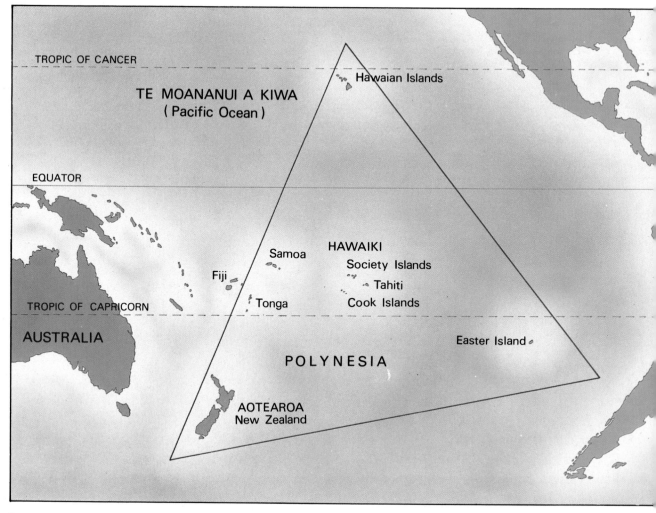

The Maoris are Polynesians, part of the great family of peoples who live in the Pacific. The islanders of Tahiti, the Cooks, Hawaii far to the north and Easter Island to the east are related to the Maoris. We know this because their languages are similar and because they look alike — medium to tall in height, well built, having brown skin and dark, wavy hair.

Many of their myths and legends are similar too, and archaeologists have found old tools and ornaments in New Zealand just like those found

They sailed in craft made from two canoes lashed together, with a cabin between for crew and provisions.

in other Polynesian islands.

Many of the canoes on which they traveled are remembered to this day. Maoris recall with pride which tribe they belong to and from which canoe's crew that tribe is descended.

It is easy to imagine groups of islanders deciding to sail off in search of a new land and a better life, just as many British people did during the nineteenth century when they, too, went to New Zealand.

A new land

These expert sailors and brave voyagers, sometimes called "the Vikings of the sunrise," set out in their canoes, leaving forever their tropical home — traditionally called Hawaiki.

Aotearoa, the Maori name for New Zealand, came as a shock to these first men and women. This new land lay outside the tropics and was a lot colder than the islands where they came from. Some of the plants they brought with them would not grow. The islands were bigger, the mountains higher and forests wilder than anything they had ever seen before.

There were very few animals — only seals, reptiles (but no snakes), and bats — so it was just as well that the first Maoris brought dogs and rats with them. But fish were plentiful and the bird life was amazing.

Many New Zealand birds cannot fly. The kiwi is the best-known example, but in those days the most important bird was the moa. Some types of moa were huge, even bigger than ostriches. Their flesh could be used for food, their bones could be carved into tools and ornaments, and the shells of their enormous eggs could even be used for carrying water.

Life on a tropical Pacific atoll (below), was very different from the wild, untamed forests and rugged mountains of New Zealand (opposite).

Ranging the forests and swamps of New Zealand, the "moa hunters" lived a peaceful, nomadic life. They discovered new edible plants and fruit-bearing trees that made their lives easier. As time passed the moa became extinct. The people worked out ways of growing crops and they began to live in villages where their numbers grew. These developments meant a big change in the Maoris' way of life.

A model of the extinct moa — some species were taller than people.

11

Chapter 2 The flowering of Maori culture

A new way of life

The Kumara is like a small knobby potato, but sweeter. The Maoris had brought some with them from Hawaiki, but it took a long time to figure out the best ways of growing and storing kumara in New Zealand. Once they solved these problems, the little kumara became the most important item in the Maori diet. It even influenced the way in which the tribes lived and organized themselves.

Families began to settle down, clearing land for farming and building villages. A family belonged to a *hapu*, or sub-tribe, and several sub-tribes made up a tribe, or *iwi*. Everyone in a tribe was related, because all were descended from the same ancestors. They all owned their land together as a tribe — nobody owned land individually. Land ownership and kinship were a matter of great pride and importance. As the tribes settled down they identified closely with the rivers, mountains and other features of their territory, all of which they regarded as sacred.

Maoris preparing food in their village. They considered that cooking was a lowly task, to be performed by women or slaves.

A rangatira *and his wife. Both are magnificently dressed when compared with the ordinary people of the tribe shown on the opposite page.*

Each tribe had its chiefs. A chief, or *rangatira*, might have more than one wife and often several slaves as well — usually prisoners captured from other tribes.

Farming made life easier for the Maoris, but it sometimes led to war. The tribes needed more territory to grow food and would fight over land as they grew in number. But even fighting was limited because all aspects of Maori life were dominated by the needs of farming, hunting and fishing.

13

Maori beliefs

The Maoris had many ideas that may seem strange to other people, in the same way that Christianity at first seemed strange to them. These ideas affected the way in which they lived.

The old tohunga *(wise man) is in a* tapu *state and must not touch cooked food, so he is being fed by a boy.*

14

We need to appreciate their ideas to understand the Maori people.

We have already seen that the Maoris had strong feelings about kinship and land. These feelings increased their *mana* — their sense of honor and prestige. *Mana* was very important to a Maori, just as honor was to a medieval knight or a Japanese samurai. It was worth dying for. It could be shared among a tribe, so glory earned by one person would be reflected on many. It also meant that an insult to one person had to be avenged by all.

Maoris were not Christians in these early times, but had their own religion with many different gods and spirits. Religion existed in all aspects of daily life, and an important belief was *tapu*. This means sacred or forbidden — the same as taboo. Certain places, objects, activities or even people might be *tapu* and had to be avoided altogether or treated with great care and respect under the direction of a *tohunga* — a sort of priest or wise man. Otherwise, the Maoris believed, terrible misfortunes and calamities would happen to them.

This may seem superstitious to many people today, but their religious attitude in life meant that the Maoris had no need for police or law courts. If someone did offend the *mana* of another person, or failed to observe a *tapu* restriction, the chief or *tohunga* soon made certain the penalty was paid.

The bones of the dead were tapu. *They were cleaned and painted and kept in a carved box like this.*

The Maoris in peace

What was it like to live in a Maori *kainga* (village) hundreds of years ago? In many ways the Maoris were lucky. The forests were full of edible birds and plants, the seas and rivers teemed with fish, and with proper care the fields yielded good crops. For tribes living in New Zealand's volcanic regions there were natural hot springs for cooking and bathing. The weather was pleasant, and the few clothes that were necessary were skillfully woven by the women from flax plants, which grew plentifully.

Children learned by watching and listening to their elders, but some boys would be selected for instruction in a special school by the *tohunga*. They would learn such aspects of Maori wisdom as history and genealogy, medicine and religion.

This huge swing was one of the devices on which the Maoris would amuse themselves.

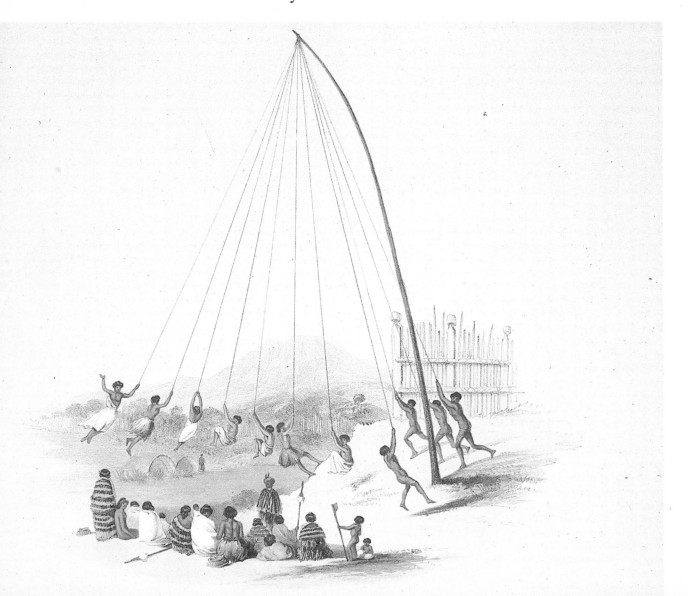

There was plenty of time to play. While the meal was cooking in the *hangi* — a kind of oven in the ground where the food cooked over hot stones — there were many games such as kite flying, top spinning or cat's cradle.

In the evening the people would gather in their reed-thatched houses and, by the light of oil lamps or the fires that kept the houses warm, they would tell stories, sing songs or recite poetry.

A warrior challenges visitors to his marae *to see if they come in peace. Others perform dances of welcome.*

Perhaps the most exciting occasions were when visitors came from another tribe. Once it was clear that the visit was peaceful, there would be much singing and dancing, speech-making and feasting. This took place on the *marae*, the central open space of the *kainga*.

The Maoris in war

Boys learned the Maori martial arts from an early age and grew up strong and agile. Their weapons were designed for hand-to-hand fighting and were used for stabbing, thrusting or clubbing. The *taiaha* was a spear-shaped weapon made of wood with a point at one end and a flat blade at the other, and could be used either as a lance or a club.

There were smaller clubs made of whalebone, wood and a kind of jade that we call greenstone. The *patu pounamu*, the greenstone club, was considered the most precious of weapons, though all were deadly when used by experienced warriors. Maoris did not use bows and arrows.

War was usually waged over land and property, but the *mana* (honor) of the tribe had to be guarded against insults of all kinds. Any such insults were avenged. The human body was considered *tapu*, the head in particular, so if a warrior ate his enemy's body or captured his head

This piece of art shows members of the tribe performing a peruperu, *or war dance.*

A Maori fortress, called a pa, *was always built with strong stockades in a well-defended position. This* pa *was built on an island, making enemy attack as difficult as possible.*

and preserved it, he increased his own *mana* while damaging that of his enemies. This might mean further war, for enemies would seek revenge (*utu*). These feuds would frequently continue for generations.

There would also be periods of peace, and enemy tribes would even join forces to fight a third enemy. Sometimes men and women from different tribes that had been at war with each other would be married in order to establish peace between the two tribes. Gifts would be exchanged and it was hoped that life would then continue normally again.

The arts of the Maori

The inside of a carved meeting house. This beautifully decorated building is now in the National Museum of New Zealand.

Art also played an important part in all aspects of Maori life. Maoris loved to decorate everything, from the tiniest fish-hooks and the leg-rings of their tame parrots to the grandest houses and mightiest war canoes. Everything they created was produced with tremendous skill and care.

Many of their art forms were unique to New Zealand. When the Maoris first arrived, their art was similar to that of other Pacific islanders. But in their new land they discovered previously unknown materials and they were able to work out new techniques of art and design. Because of these new techniques, Maori art is quite different from any other in the world.

Carving was the art of the men, and weaving was the art of the women. These two arts came together in the best houses belong-

20

ing to chiefs and other important people. The walls of these houses were lined with intricate carvings of ancestors, interspersed with beautifully patterned woven panels.

This intricate carving is a self-portrait by the carver Rahurir Rukupo, who built the house shown on the opposite page.

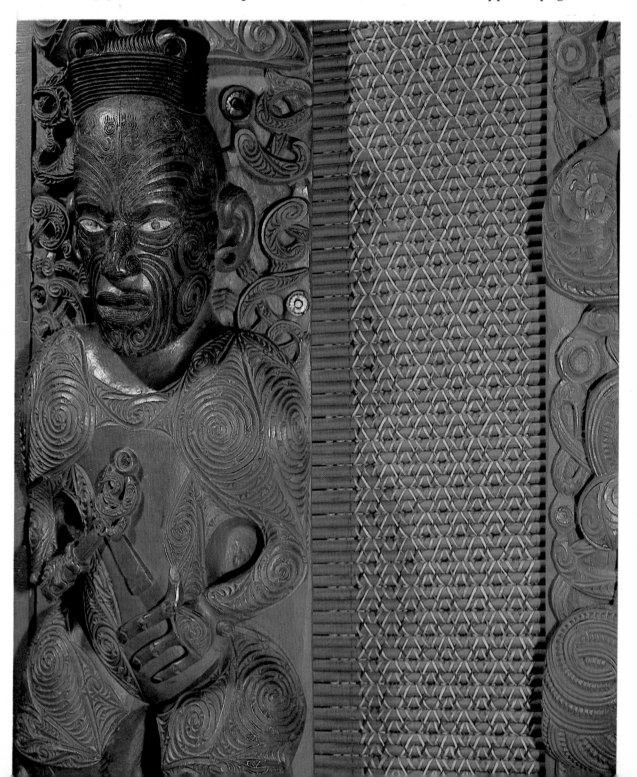

Carving and weaving

Using only stone tools, Maori men produced some of the most intricate carving the world has ever seen. They devised elaborate patterns of swirling spirals interwoven with wriggling monsters. They would apply these designs to weapons, treasure boxes, canoes, flutes, tools and houses. Even the stockades of the *pa* (fortress) were decorated with fearsome carvings to frighten away enemies.

The Maoris even carved their own bodies. Like many peoples of the world, they were fond of tattooing. The Maoris carved patterns into their skin with tiny chisels — an extremely painful process. Men had more tattooing on their faces than women, and they also tattooed their thighs and buttocks. Although the last tattooed man died over fifty years ago, there are still a few old and respected women still living whose lips and chins are tattooed in the old way.

This portrait of the imposing chief Ihaka Whaanga clearly shows the intricate designs tattooed on his face.

Weaving cloaks from flax fiber and dogskin was painstaking work because the Maoris had no looms, but the results were beautiful.

The women wove from the various types of flax and other plants that grow in New Zealand. They made baskets, floor mats, sandals, simple clothes and more elaborate cloaks that were often decorated with feathers, dog fur or intricate zig-zag patterns.

Greenstone, which the Maoris call *pounamu*, was a useful discovery. It is an extremely hard kind of jade found on New Zealand's South Island. The Maoris had no knowledge of metals so they used greenstone for their axes, chisels, weapons and ornaments. These weapons might take many years to make, and so were highly prized. Special names were given to these weapons, and they were handed down from generation to generation.

Chapter 3 The coming of the Pakeha

The impact of the settlers

The Maoris had to face great challenges in Aotearoa, as they called New Zealand. They overcame the difficulties of working with new methods in everything from art to agriculture, and evolved a way of life that was perfectly suited to their new country.

The picture of a Pakeha bartering with a Maori for a crayfish was painted by an English sailor.

Even greater challenges had to be faced with the arrival of white people, who were called Pakehas. A Dutchman, Abel Tasman, visited New Zealand in 1642. However, it was not until James Cook, an English captain, arrived with an expedition in 1769 that real contact was made between the races.

The Pakehas were a mixed blessing. Although they brought strange and wonderful ideas and materials — iron, cloth, pottery, new

These chiefs were taken to England by the missionary (right) but one returned to New Zealand with firearms to slaughter his enemies.

animals and crops — they also brought diseases that the Maoris had never before known and to which they had no natural immunity. Whites also brought with them alcohol and firearms. The first Pakehas to live in New Zealand were a rough, tough crowd. They were escaped convicts from Australia, seamen from visiting whaling and trading ships, and a few adventurers.

In 1814 the first Christian missionaries arrived. The Maoris were not impressed by Christianity at first — they preferred their own religion. However they tolerated and cared for the missionaries, who taught them to read and write, showed them new foods, and brought all kinds of goods that made life easier — iron for tools, weapons and fish-hooks, woolen blankets and clothes. The old way of life was about to change forever.

Subjects of the Queen

New Zealand in the early nineteenth century was like the American Wild West. There was no law to control the Pakehas who were living mainly in the north. Among the Maoris, the *tohungas* and *rangatiras* found it increasingly difficult to control their people. The changes proved very disruptive to Maori society.

Meanwhile, colonists continued to arrive from Britain looking for land to settle. They were able to buy land cheaply from the Maoris, who did not understand that these new-comers intended to keep this land for themselves forever. This custom of land ownership was strange to the Maoris.

Eventually the British Government was persuaded to step in and end the confusion. In 1840, an agreement called the Treaty of Waitangi was signed between a representative of Queen Victoria and a few Maori chiefs. The chiefs relinquished their power to the Queen in return for guarantees regarding their land and property, and protection under British law.

New Zealand became part of the

A chief addresses his warriors before they set off to war in their canoes. Most of them are armed with muskets.

The Pakehas' influence was not always destructive. For instance, they taught the Maoris new ways of farming.

British Empire. The Treaty did not work well, however. Many chiefs did not understand it, especially the British idea of sovereignty; others refused to sign it altogether; and frequently the British ignored it. Maori land was still disappearing and some Maoris felt they were worse off than before. Fighting broke out between Maoris and Pakehas in the 1840s — in Wellington and the Bay of Islands — and the Maoris lost. However, there were even worse times to come.

The land wars

By the 1860s, the Maoris were outnumbered by Pakeha settlers, who demanded more and more land for themselves. Despite the Treaty of Waitangi, the Government was on the side of the settlers, and the Maoris were regarded by many as primitive nuisances.

Some North Island chiefs realized they would have to fight for their land. Already a few important tribes had joined together and elected their own king to lead them, a chief who had refused to sign the treaty.

In 1860, fighting broke out in

A party of Maoris ambush Pakeha soldiers as they cross a stream in the bush. The Maoris excelled at guerrilla fighting in the dense New Zealand forests.

Taranaki over fertile land that the Pakehas wanted. This was the excuse the Government needed to go to war and take over the land they wanted. Government troops invaded the Waikato, which was another region like Taranaki with good farmland. The fighting continued until the Maori leaders were defeated, one by one.

As a result, more than 3 million acres of land were confiscated from Maori tribes that had defied the Government.

Outnumbered and ill-equipped, the Maoris had little chance of winning. The tribes were not united — some fought on the Government side. For a while the New Zealanders even had the help of troops sent over from Britain. However, many of the British soldiers did not like fighting the Maoris. They respected them and thought the wars were unfair.

This period is still remembered with great bitterness by the Maoris. Their feelings are that the Pakehas were unjust in attacking them. The Maoris lost not only many men, women and children and much of their territory in the fighting, they also lost their *mana*.

Maori prisoners of war under guard on a prison ship in Wellington harbor.

King Tawhiao withdrew with his people into a region still known today as the King Country. In this territory they were left alone by the Government.

A dying race

Not all the tribes had been involved in the wars, and some suffered worse than others. In general, the years following the fighting of the 1860s and 1870s were a bad time for all the Maori people. They were still losing their land because of new laws. Most of them were so poor that even if they still had their farms they could not afford to develop them. They were not able to borrow money as the Pakeha farmers were.

Some of the Maori people decided to turn their backs on the new world. They formed communities around new leaders. These were prophets who mixed old Maori ideas and beliefs with parts of the Bible and created new religions. Such groups wanted to be left alone in peace, but the Government frequently sent forces to disperse them.

Like the Indians of North America and the Aborigines of Australia, the Maoris land had also been taken by foreigners. The Maoris, as a race, became withdrawn and isolated. Living in poverty and bad conditions, and suffering terrible epidemics of European diseases, their population was getting smaller. By 1900 there were little more than 40,000 Maoris left. It was thought that they were a dying race and would soon disappear altogether, as did the Aborigines of Tasmania, who had been wiped out after the arrival of white settlers.

Some of the bleakness and despair of those hard years is captured in this old photograph taken in the King Country.

However, the Maoris had adapted to new challenges in the past and they would continue to do so in the future. Instead of opposing the world of the Pakeha, they began to become a part of it, while at the same time making sure that they continued to hold on to their own unique traditions.

Chapter 4 **The Maoris today**

Into the twentieth century

From the gloomy years at the end of the nineteenth century, the Maori people began to make a recovery. New chiefs emerged with talents adapted to coping with the new world. Among them were Sir Apirana Ngata, a politician who encouraged his people to hold on to their ancient culture and at the same time learn the skills of the Pakehas. Sir Maui Pomare was also a politician and a doctor who did much to improve the health of his people. T.W. Ratana founded a new Maori branch of Christianity and forged links with the Labour Party of New Zealand. Although there had been four Maori Members of Parliament (MPs) since 1867, Maori influence on politics had never been as strong as it became by the 1930s.

Sir Apirana Ngata, a much-respected leader of the Maori people.

Women played a more conspicuous role at both tribal and national levels. They had their own famous leaders such as Te Puea Herangi and Whina Cooper. A Maori Women's Welfare League was founded, which is still influential in government policy.

In both world wars, Maori troops fought alongside other Commonwealth contingents, and the Maori Battalion of World War II won a proud reputation as a fighting force.

World War II also meant big changes for the Maoris who stayed at home. More people were required to

Troops of the Maori Battalion en route to Italy, during World War II.

work in industry, and Maoris gradually began to move away from their traditional homes in the country and into the towns and cities of New Zealand. This was to become a migration as important as the epic canoe journeys of 1,000 years before — a vital change not only for the Maoris but also for the rest of New Zealand.

Maoris in modern New Zealand

In many ways the Maoris are just like any other New Zealanders today. Most of them live in the cities. They wear the same kinds of clothes and live in the same kinds of houses as anyone else. They go to school or to work like anyone else, too. All except a few old people speak English. There has been so much intermarriage that many people with Maori ancestry look like Pakehas and have European surnames.

New Zealand has enjoyed a good reputation for its race relations, and the many different immigrant races and native Maoris get along well together. In fact, certain laws and organizations, such as the Government's Department of Maori Affairs, exist to help Maoris.

Visitors to New Zealand are usually impressed by what they see of Maori life, a colorful and attractive spectacle in the tourist centers where people can attend concerts and banquets and learn a little of how the Maoris lived long ago. People in other countries may be familiar with Maori art in museums, may have admired the

The famous Maori All Blacks rugby team in action.

A girl poses in traditional Maori costume by a carved gateway at a popular tourist center.

Maoris' skill at rugby, or know of such famous people as Kiri Te Kanawa, the Maori opera singer.

So it would seem that there are very few differences between the Maoris and the Pakehas in New Zealand, and that today everything works to the Maoris' advantage. However. there *are* still many differences. In certain important respects, life for the Maoris is not always as easy as it appears to be.

Protest!

The loss of so much of their land still angers many Maoris, and in recent years there have been several protests. Two are illustrated on these pages.

Loss of land is not their only problem. Statistics show that most Maoris live in worse homes, have a poorer education, commit more crimes, are more likely to be unemployed, and die younger than Pakehas. This is not because they are more lazy, stupid or primitive than whites, but because for too long they

The Maori Land March took place in 1975, when thousands walked across the country to demonstrate against the loss of their land.

Some Maoris squatted on land that they believed to be theirs: the land was sold and the issue is still a source of grievance.

have had to fit into a way of life that was never designed to suit them. This new lifestyle shows little respect for the ideas and feelings of the Maoris themselves. For a long time the Maori language was banned in schools, for example. Maoris have had to adjust to tremendous changes in a short time and, on many occasions, Pakehas have regarded them and their culture as inferior. This often happens when one race is overwhelmed by another. Blacks in the United States and Britain, Aborigines in Australia, and Indians and Eskimos of North America have found themselves faced with some of the same problems.

Today the Maoris are fighting back. Although the Government has made some attempts to improve their situation, there are protest groups who feel that progress is too slow and that the Maoris are still not able to participate fully in the life of New Zealand. They want an end to the racism that still exists in their country. They see the Treaty of Waitangi as a hopeless muddle — or even a big fraud. In all areas of life, such as education, the media, politics, health, employment, they want a fair share for themselves. They also want more freedom to observe their own customs and more respect for their culture from Pakehas.

Chapter 5 The Maori renaissance

Maoritanga

As Maoris realize how much of their culture has been lost, they are determined to hang on to what remains. Because of this, there has been an upsurge of interest in *Maoritanga* — "Maoriness," or the Maori way of doing things — which has been described as a Maori renaissance.

Today, many thousands of Maoris brought up to speak only English are now learning their own language and rediscovering the old arts of weaving, carving, singing, dancing and oratory. They are showing new interest in their tribal origins, traditions and legends. Meeting houses are springing up all over New Zealand, carved and decorated to reflect the pride of the communities they serve. Such community centers are now often built right in cities for all Maoris — not just a particular tribe — and for Pakehas too. Maori gatherings (*huis*) are attended in greater numbers than ever before. A *hui* may be attended by thousands, with tribal groups arriving from all parts of New Zealand.

Maoritanga is not just what is seen or heard. It includes old values like *whanaungatanga* (family relation-

A scene at the Maori Arts and Crafts Institute where the old skills of flax weaving and wood carving are taught.

ships) and *aroha* (love, sympathy and caring). Many Maoris find the Pakeha view of life narrow and selfish, and prefer living and working in cooperation with other Maoris.

The hongi, *the traditional form of greeting between Maoris.*

The marae

On page 17 we saw how visitors from one tribe to another were welcomed on the *marae*, or open space in the village. This is one of the customs that has survived right into the present day.

Today the word *marae* has a slightly different meaning, and includes not only the open space but also the buildings grouped around it to form a kind of community center. This is a big meeting house and other buildings for dining, cooking, showers and toilets.

A present day warrior performs the wero, *challenging visitors arriving at his* marae.

Young Maoris enjoy themselves at a hui. *Some are wearing dreadlocks and relate to the black culture of the United States, Britain and the Caribbean.*

A large number of people can stay at a *marae* for several days, and it is the scene for many Maori *huis*. A *hui* may be a wedding or a conference, a political meeting or, most important, a *tangi*. This is a Maori funeral, which usually lasts three days. A *tangi* is important, not only as an occasion when visitors from near and far can pay their respects to the dead but also because it sums up all of the most powerful features of *Maoritanga*. Language, religion and custom come together in a uniquely

Maori way, and for a few days on the *marae* the bustle of the outside world can be forgotten.

Other *huis* are more cheerful, colorful affairs. There are speeches, singing and dancing, the opportunity to catch up with old friends and make new ones, and share food cooked in the traditional way — in the *hangi*.

Gatherings help to make sure that *Maoritanga* lives on, and Maoris will often say that a *hui* helps them to "recharge their batteries."

The Maori language

Throughout this book we have seen a number of Maori words. They look strange to people outside New Zealand. Even within New Zealand most people have difficulty saying them properly. This even applies to some Maoris because for years deliberate attempts were made to suppress the language. Maori schoolchildren could have been punished if they were caught speaking in their own language.

Maori elders delight in making speeches, and their oratory is expressed in rich and colorful language.

Times are slowly changing, and New Zealanders are beginning to realize that to neglect or misuse the Maori language is an insult to Maoris and their culture, and that to encourage the language is good, for Maoris and for New Zealand as a whole. Today Maori is not banned in schools. It can be taught at the secondary level. Parents can send their very young children to a *kohanga reo*, a kind of kindergarten where Maori is spoken. In that way a young child can learn Maori and English together. On television, the newsreaders and weather forecasters — usually Pakehas — try to pronounce Maori place names correctly.

The Maori language sounds different depending on the tribe of the speaker, but there are some basic rules that will help you to pronounce the Maori words in this book.

* The vowels — a, e, i, o, u — are usually pronounced as in but, bet, bit, bought, boot.
* If two vowels come together, each is pronounced separately even if the word is said quickly. Thus *moa* is not pronounced as in the word mow or mower but almost as in more (mo-a).
* The consonants — h, k, m, n, p, r, t, w, wh, ng — are much the same as in English except for the last two. The letters wh are usually said as "f," while ng is pronounced as in the middle of singing, not tango.

Young Maori children at a kohanga reo *where they learn to speak their native language.*

The Maoris in the future

A hundred years ago it was thought that the Maoris were dying out, but today there are more than ever before. This shows how difficult it is to look into the future!

One thing is certain. The Maori people will continue to strive for equality with their Pakeha neighbors. They do not want to be the same as Pakehas — which would destroy their *Maoritanga* — but they want the same freedom as Pakehas have. Much has happened in recent years to advance this process. Many Maoris — young and old, men and women — are working in their own ways to make New Zealand a better country for future generations of Maoris.

Surrounded by Maori elders and youngsters, world-famous rock star David Bowie takes a keen interest in the proceedings at a marae *in Wellington.*

The Treaty of Waitangi Protest in 1984, when thousands of Maoris converged on Waitangi to express their concern about their problems and future prospects.

Gradually, Pakehas are beginning to realize the fairness of Maori demands. Not only do they feel guilty about the way Maoris have been treated in the past, and about the impoverished lives so many lead in the present, but they also realize that Maori culture can benefit New Zealand.

New Zealand's historic links with Britain are weakening, and it is obvious that the country's future is as a Pacific nation and not as a European one. So it is not surprising that New Zealanders are gradually waking up to the distinctive culture of the Maoris, which helps give their country its special flavor and character.

Changes happen slowly — too slowly for some Maoris. They have faced up to challenges before, and it is to be hoped that the Maori people will play a much larger part in the New Zealand of the future than they have been allowed to do so far.

45

Glossary

Aborgines The original native people of Australia.

Archaeologist Someone who looks for and studies the remains of an ancient culture in order to learn how people used to live.

Atoll A circular coral island enclosing a lagoon.

Epidemic A widespread outbreak of disease.

Eskimos A race of people living in the far north of Alaska, Canada, Greenland and Siberia.

Extinct When an animal or plant species has died out and no longer exists.

Genealogy The study of how families are descended from and related to each other.

Grievance A reason for complaint.

Immunity The ability to resist a disease.

Kinship The links between people who are related to one another.

Kiwi A bird that cannot fly, native to New Zealand.

Kumara A small, sweet potato.

Migration To move in a group, from one country to another.

Missionary Someone who travels to another country to convert the natives there to a different religion. In this case, Christian missionaries sent to convert the Maoris to Christianity.

Moa A large, sometimes enormous, flightless bird. It used to live in New Zealand, but has now become extinct.

Nomadic Moving from place to place to find food.

Oratory The art of public speaking. Among the Maoris, someone who can make a fine public speech, an orator, is regarded with great respect.

Racism An aggressive attitude by members of one race toward another.

Renaissance A revival or rebirth of a culture, originally used in Europe to describe the period following the "Dark Ages."

Samurai A Japanese warrior.

Sovereignty The supreme power and authority of a state.

Taboo Disapproved of or forbidden.

Books to read

Models of Society: Class, Stratification and Gender in Australia and New Zealand by Frank Jones and Peter Davis (Croom Helm, 1986)

The Fern and the Tiki by David P. Ausubel (Chris Mass, 1977)

We Live in New Zealand by John Ball (Watts, 1984)

Religion in New Zealand Society by Brian Colless and Peter Donovan (Fortress, 1980)

The New Zealanders: How They Live and Work by R.J. Johnson (H. Holt and Co., 1976)

Call Back Yesterday: A New Zealand Idyll by Ralph Richardson (Book Guild Ltd., 1986)

Colonization of New Zealand by Johannes S. Marais (AMS Press, 1972)

Maori Myths and Legends by Roger Hart and A.W. Reed (A.H. & A.W. Reed, 1983)

Glossary of Maori words

Aroha Love, sympathy and caring.

Haka A warlike dance performed with aggressive movements, gestures and grimaces.

Hangi An oven dug in the ground where food is cooked over hot stones.

Hapu A sub-tribe.

Hawaiki The legendary Polynesian island home of the first Maori settlers.

Heitiki An ornament carved from greenstone, which was worn around the neck.

Hui A gathering of people or a celebration.

Iwi A tribe.

Kainga Maori village.

Kohanga reo Literally a "language nest," a kind of kindergarten where young children go to learn the Maori language.

Mana The Maori sense of honor and prestige.

Maoritanga The Maori way of life, or "Maoriness."

Marae Originally the central open space in a Maori *kainga*. Nowadays a *marae* includes buildings grouped around an open space and serves as a community center.

Pa A fortress, or fortified village, surrounded by a stockade. They were always built in a well-defended position, such as on a hilltop.

Pakeha A white person.

Patu pounamu A greenstone club, considered the most precious of weapons.

Peruperu A war dance.

Pounamu Maori name for greenstone — a kind of jade found in the South Island of New Zealand.

Rangatira A chief in a tribe.

Taiaha A long weapon with a sharp point at one end and a flat blade at the other.

Tangi A sorrow, a funeral.

Tapu Something that is sacred and forbidden.

Tohunga A priest or wise man.

Utu Repayment or revenge.

Wero A warrior's challenge to visitors to the *marae*.

Whanaungatanga Family relationships.

Picture acknowledgments

Alexander Turnbull Library, Wellington 7, 9, 12, 13, 16, 17, 19, 25, 26, 27, 29, 30, 32, 33; Auckland City Art Gallery 15, 22, 23; Auckland Institute and Museum 28; British Library 24; Peter Bush 34; Department of Maori Affairs 2, 36, 37, 39, 40, 41, 42, 43, 44, 48; Department of Maori Studies, Victoria University, Wellington 31; National Museum of New Zealand 6 (lower), 11 (lower), 14, 18, 20, 21; National Publicity Studio of New Zealand 10, 11 (upper), 35; Wayland Picture Library 38, 39. Maps on pages 6 and 8 by Bill Donohoe. Cover picture by Axel Poignant. Picture research by Philip Whaanga.

Index